DECALOGUE

THE FIRST ATTEMPT AT FORMULATING
UNIVERSAL LAWS
And Metamorphosing Energy

EXEGESIS
by
Stanisław Kapuściński

ℍℙ
PUBLISHED BY INHOUSEPRESS

For all my
Friends
who are still searching

THE DECALOGUE
TEN COMMANDMENTS
Exodus 20: 3-17
In Search of Secular Ethics

EXEGESIS

We might regard the Decalogue as the first attempt to define the *Universal Laws*, which assure a life of happiness in the phenomenal reality. Moses had a choice. He could attempt to create a substitute religion for the 2000 gods the Egyptians produced to populate their Pantheon, or to attempt to free his people from the plethora of false images, idolatry and subservience to the powerful priesthood, by opening his people's minds to the potential within them.

He concluded that it must have been an incredible Creative Energy that made him, that gave him awareness, the ability to think of new concepts, such as freeing his people from slavery. As there was no one else around, he concluded that this power, this ability must rest within his own self.

He realized that for as long as his people didn't start

thinking for themselves, rather than following other people's concepts, they'll remain slaves not only in their bodies, but also in their minds.

That was the starting point.

He must have concluded that to set his people free he must liberate their minds, and even their emotions. To do so, they needed some guidelines for living. For becoming more than they were at present. He had to place the concept of the Creative Energy, of the Creative Force, within them.

First and foremost, Moses must have committed himself to free peoples' minds. His commandments were suggestions of what might set them free. There were no punishments for breaking them. There were only consequences.

The rest is history.

Poor Moses. In 13th century BCE he delivered his people from Egyptian slavery. Yet, presumably out of ignorance or dire stupidity, his teaching has been studiously ignored ever since.

Actually, it was neither stupidity nor ignorance; at least, not in the normal sense.

It was Ego.

Not Moses' of course, only the exulted faith in the intelligence generated by the brain of his primitive followers. The same problem threw us out of Eden. Sadly, to this day, we are all still suffering from the same misconceptions. Particularly from the weakness and perversion of pride. Look at our past or present leaders. Do they not think of themselves as better than others? As superior human beings? Do they remind you of anyone?

Nothing has changed.

After Moses, the Hebrew Prophets, finally Yeshûa, and eventually s few of the later saints, met with the same abnegation. They all met with exactly the same lack of recognition as Moses. We, humans, must be the most ungrateful species that ever evolved out of stardust. Or... perhaps, we haven't evolved at all? Our bodies have, but the use of our potential appears to have remained at a standstill. Perhaps, just perhaps, there may have been a time when we had been smart, or smarter, and gradually, over millennia, we lost our perspicacity. We became material beings, guided in our Becoming by the artificial intelligence generated by our brains.

That's right. Our magnificent brains are capable of generating artificial intelligence.

The so-called, AI.

They have their purpose. In fact, two of them. One— their job is to keep us alive in the phenomenal reality. And two—is to generate diversity in this very same phenomenal Universe, and hence, to contribute to its continuous expansion.

Regrettably, the rest of us, other than the Few that were chosen [1], are also still regressing from the bliss of Paradise. The bliss of the Garden of Eden. In addition, we seem bent on destroying our immune system in many ways. We overeat, we don't exercise our bodies; we even pollute our air to cause our lungs and hearts to dysfunction long before their assigned time. The eleven major organ systems in the human body, which took millions if not billions of years to develop, were, and still are, ignored. Most of us do not appear to be even aware of them all.

And all this, because we had chosen, and continue to choose, to ignore "mother nature". Nature that is guided by the Universal Laws, which Moses attempted to re-instill in our minds. And... he failed.

And once again, we might ask...

WHY?

And the answer is staggering.

It is because a group of people wanted to control our minds. Our behaviour. To control us. And how, you might ask?

By converting Mosaic teaching into a religion.

And how could those people assure our obedience? That's easy. Every religion relies on the carrot and the stick doctrine. Both, leaders of religions and dictators used it throughout history. In religions, however, in order to assure ab*solute obedience,* the carrot and the stick must also be absolute. *Heaven and Hell* seemed like a good alternative to Eden. And *sinners* were so much easier to control than people who were *aspiring gods*. No matter what Moses showed us, what prophets had said, what Jesus repeated. [1]

All dictators, religious and secular, can only control people through fear. The ignorant masses must never be reminded that they are all "gods in waiting". Gods with absolute potential to manipulate reality with their will. With ability to metamorphose energy in the phenomenal Universe.

To perform 'miracles' by the act of their will.

Our will. The power is dormant within every one of us. We are not all born equal, but we are all born with equal potential.

Good luck!

We really shouldn't have eaten that apple! After all, little knowledge is a dangerous thing. And the less knowledge we had, the easier we were to manipulate.

And thus, slowly yet persistently, we have become part of the illusion of the illusory phenomenal Universe.

This is not religion.

This is science.

No matter. Hopefully the cycle will change.

Soon.

After all, we're entering the A*ge of Aquarius*. The age of the individual?

To continue. Our brains have evolved, but not our ability to use them. It is like modern music. The instruments are still great, but fewer and fewer of us know how to play them. Likewise our minds and bodies have evolved into magnificent instruments of creativity. Already in the day of ancient Egypt their magicians were capable of metamorphosing illusions before our very eyes. They didn't match Moses' abilities, but they were aware of the potential within them.

And Moses, we seem to have forgotten, was the greatest magician of them all. He had proven this by metamorphosing the energy of which all 'things' are made no less then 42 times. [1] At least that many 'miracles' have been describe in the Torah. Forty-two times he manipulated reality until the rulers of Egypt became afraid to keep him amongst them. They let him and his people go. Such was the power of just one man. The power that lies dormant in every one of us. That's right. Within you and me. All we need to learn to use it. [2]

If we are to believe our scientists, notably Albert Einstein, our reality is an illusion, although he admits: *"a very persistent one"*. So persistent that we, as a species, forgot our origins.

Remember Eden?

A garden so beautiful that we referred to it as Paradise? That was our state of Consciousness. Yet, we are very good at forgetting. We had lots of practice. Yet, Albert Einstein assures us that:

"All is Energy",
and
"Energy Cannot Be Destroyed!"

Hence, as we, too, are energy, no matter what we do, we, the real we, cannot be destroyed. That, my friends, makes us immortal.

Our bodies are not. Our blood cells might live for just 13 days. The top layer of our skin sticks around for up to 30 days. Our red blood cells might last for 120 days. That's it. We are constantly changing. Metamorphosing.

We are not real.

So why do we identify with other bodies?

We even ignore the teaching of the FEW amongst us.

We always did. That's our nature. Actually, it is not us who are stupid. It is the artificial intelligence generated by our brains.

Moses tried to change that.

He's still trying... He'd given us some hints. Ten of them. Remember? We call them the *Ten Commandments*, and then promptly ignore them. To this very day nobody follows them. Nobody listened. Like in the day of Moses.

Well, almost nobody listens. The overwhelming majority.

I'll list them below with some notes to make them easier to understand. After all Moses delivered them quite a while ago. Things change. Customs change. Our science has grown. Only our character stayed behind.

~~~~

THE
TEN COMMANDMENTS

1
"Thou shalt have no other gods before me."

To gain even a rudimentary understanding of this commandment, we must ask who is "me", who are "other gods", and who is speaking to whom. Moses, who purportedly offered this statement to his people, was alone on Mount Sinai. He never spoke of any other beings, extraterrestrial or otherwise. Luckily for us, in Genesis 3:14, when Moses had been asked who is "me", the name of God, he heard an explicit answer: I AM THAT I AM stressing "this is my name for ever..."

This attests to our duality.

Moses, as indeed everyone of us, is of dual nature. Our consciousness consists of Being (the eternal Self), and Becoming (the transient phenomenal entity).

The first is the Individualization of the Omnipresent Consciousness, the second is the phenomenal creation of this Creative Energy, which resulted in our brains generating artificial intelligence, which we all know as our Ego.

Thus Moses spoke and listened to his Higher Self, his true Self, and hence he attributed all his statements to God (to repeat: to the Individualization of the Omnipresent Consciousness.) And indeed, we all have the capacity to reach into our unconscious and discover that we are more than flesh and bones.

According to Moses, our true, or higher Self is the

only God we are allowed to recognize, let alone worship. He calls IT: the I AM. However, under no circumstances are we allowed to confuse IT with our Ego. In fact, in the ability to differentiate between the two lies the secret of our immortality.

Ego is transient. I AM is immortal.

It's a simple at that.

And under no circumstances are we allowed to worship any divinity, any power, any 'energy', other than that which exists *within* us. We are not to have ANY OTHER Gods before the I AM. Before the Divine Energy that has created us in ITS own image and likeness. But, to repeat again, we must make abundantly sure that we do not confuse this Divinity, this Creative Energy, this Individualization of the Omnipresent Consciousness, with our Ego. Or with any other real or imagined idol, purporting to be the Creative Energy. There is but One God, and the Higher Self, the I AM, is ITS only expression accessible to us.

This is the first and the most profound Commandment of all. And why?

Because in essence, our true Self and the Omnipresent Consciousness are ONE. We are inseparable individualizations of the Omnipresent Consciousness. Of that which the atheists call God!

2
"Thou shalt not make unto thee any graven image, or any likeness of any thing that is in heaven above, or that is in the earth beneath, or that is in the water under the earth."

Why? Because, in essence, our true Self and the Omnipresent Consciousness are ONE.

> *"Thou shalt not bow down thyself to them, nor serve them: for I the LORD thy God am a jealous God, visiting the iniquity of the fathers upon the children unto the third and fourth generation of them that hate me; And showing mercy unto thousands of them that love me, and keep my commandments."*
>
> (Exodus 20:5)

This statement, unfortunately, destroys all architecture connected to any religion originating in Judeo-Christian traditions. I said unfortunately, because while it negates the concept of the only temple/church/public gathering connected in any way to our contact with the 'divine', is to take place exclusively within our minds and hearts.

And yet, the churches can be regarded not so much a places of worship, but as museums of quite exemplary artworks, inspired by the contact with our Creative Consciousness. Thus they enhance the beauty of the phenomenal universe. If treated as such, they would be very welcome. If treated as 'exclusive' places of worship, then they'd do more harm than good. The temple of Higher Self, of I AM, is within, not without. This has been taught by ALL Prophets of yore. This teaching has been ignored for thousands of years.

Regretfully, such gross misinterpretation of ancient teaching began with King David and his son, Solomon, and has been perpetrated by the sacerdotal groups who wished to maintain control over the minds of people.

There appears to be ample "Evidence The Temple Was NOT God's Will" [3]

And yet, the temple built by Solomon on plans prepared by David were the beginning of "Earthly Kingdom", as against Kingdom NOT of the world. As again, the eternal Kingdom Within, not the transient kingdom without. Everything, every pearl of wisdom taught by the Prophets, dealt with our 'inner' reality. Unfortunately, Paul in contrast to St. Peter, sided with the earthy kingdom.

There is a reason for this, but regrettably, the Israelites took another millennium to find out why. The reason, of course, was that already Moses had been attempting to build a "Kingdom NOT of this world". And only Yeshûa reminded them about it in as many words.

We, "Christians" still seem to remain deaf.

Perhaps for Moses it may have been easier. He may have been inspired by the abundance of 'gods' in the religion of Egypt. After all, they exceeded most other religions with more than 2000 deities. That's a lot of gods to worship, be grateful to, or even... on occasion, to blame for one's misfortunes.

It seems that Moses not only wanted to free his people from reliance on the munificence of outside influences, but to encourage, if not enforce, reliance upon their own resources, let alone their ultimate potential. From the evolutionary point of view, this was a tremendous step forward.

Yet, regrettably, his people were not ready.

He took 40 years trying to plant the seed before he'd given up. Our subconscious is a stubborn lady. Like Eve?

As a matter of fact, the overwhelming majority of people are not ready to accept Mosaic teaching to this very day. We still pray to some imaginary entity, "up above the clouds", rather then reaching deep within our own Consciousness to discover our infinite potential.

Imagine — Moses, a number of Prophets, Yeshûa, a multitude of saints... and people still flock to images displayed on the altars, or the promises affirmed by television preachers.

And yet the only power they'll ever witness will be, or would be, the power churning within them. Our Egos, the artificial intelligence generated by our brain, seem to refuse to play second fiddle.

3
"Thou shalt not take the name of the LORD thy God in vain; for the LORD will not hold him guiltless that taketh his name in vain."

This is a fantastic foresight into the future. Here Moses quite evidently appears to be aware of the power of the creative energy of thought.

When we invoked certain images, or even certain concepts, the rate of vibration of such thoughts appeared to attract similar vibrations from our phenomenal reality. Hence we must be very careful what thoughts we entertain in our consciousness. Love, attracts the vibrations of love. Hate, the rate of vibrations of hate. The word murder has similar 'magnetic' properties. We must be very careful what we think. Our reality is the sum-total of our thoughts.

It seems that Moses knew that. Most of us still do not. Yet the total thoughts generated by humanity result in the reality of our phenomenal world.

Perhaps that's why we are, at present, in such a mess? (Don't worry too much—our reality is an illusion. We can change it).

4
Remember the Sabbath day, to keep it holy.

Marks and Engels would be please with this commandment. Particularly, the rest of the Commandment:

> *"Six days shalt thou labor, and do all thy work:*
> *But the seventh day is the Sabbath of the LORD*
> *thy God: in it thou shalt not do any work, thou,*
> *nor thy son, nor thy daughter, thy manservant,*
> *nor thy maidservant, nor thy cattle, nor thy*
> *stranger that is within thy gates: For in six days*
> *the LORD made heaven and earth, the sea, and*
> *all that is in them, and rested the seventh day:*
> *wherefore the LORD blessed the Sabbath day,*
> *and hallowed it."*

(Exodus 20:9)

Needless to day, it has nothing whatsoever to do with the relationship of our Ego to our Self. I strongly suspect that the whole Commandment has been put in for the sole purpose of attracting the masses, the "simple folk" to the concept of accepting the other "Universal Laws". We can hardly blame Moses for this. After all he'd just led his people, until recently enslaved, to face the concept of monotheism. He had to make it attractive. After all, most people must have been afraid of the wrath of the thousands of gods they'd just left behind. I'd strongly suspect that their masters of yesterday did their best to dissuade them from choosing freedom for the completely unknown.

The concept of the Sabbath day has been retained in the Christian religion that followed some centuries later. It seems that we can do whatever we want for the rest of the week, providing we deliver our tithes to the priesthood on the seventh day.

This, of course, has nothing to do with Universal Laws, or with any laws bearing slightest resemblance to spiritual life. Something must have happened when Moses dropped the stone tablets the first time... although, perhaps, the first tablets may have been too hard to swallow?

Or it could be, that in slavery the workers didn't have a single day off and Moses decided that that's the least he can do for them.

For all of them.

For their masters, their children, or even their maids and menservants. That was probably the only way he could think of attracting ALL his people to the new philosophy of life, let alone from the relative and precarious security of freedom. Frankly, that's the least he could have done.

Yet, it seems to work to this day, although nothing else does. The other Commandments have been studiously ignored.

So much for metaphysics.

For a while now, I continued to share with you my contentions that the scriptures of Judeo-Christian religion have absolutely nothing whatsoever to do with any religion. They teach people how to be healthy, happy, and live a long and productive life. In other words to get back as close as they can to the Garden of Eden.

To get back to Paradise that awaits us within.

The rest is up to us.

5

Honor thy father and thy mother: that thy days may be long upon the land which the LORD thy God giveth thee.

If Moses suspected that all too soon he might need the assistance of his people to keep his body and soul together, his concern for honoring the elders, was the only way to assure his future. While this does not sound very religious, Universal Laws seldom do. They are not concerned with individuals but rather with the whole species, which reflects the success of evolution.

On the other hand, this Commandment may have been inspired by the behaviour of his own children. The Book of Exodus mentions his wife, Zipporah (or Tzipora), and his two sons, Gershom and Eliezer, who might have not behaved appropriately.

This last suggestion seems the more likely.

After all, Moses was of advanced consciousness, but he was still human. And, in spite of his prophetic abilities, he couldn't have known that he would not reach the Promised Land. Although, from the metaphysical point of view, Promised Land is a state of consciousness, and in this Moses exceed all his compatriots.

6
"Thou shalt not kill."

The 6th Commandment is by far most grossly misunderstood.

It is not just that when we kill a man or a woman we actually murder someone's beloved child, their son or daughter, but that we are an integral part of what he or she was. Has been. The physical body, which we destroy is the temporary domicile of an individualization of the Omnipresent Consciousness, which created, built and developed that body for a purpose. We had nothing to do with its creation, hence we have no right to destroy it. If we are of a truly limited intelligence than we probably don't realized that it took millions of years to develop an entity consisting of billions of cells working in perfect harmony.

Yes, that is our temporal home. Billions of cells working in perfect harmony.

We are constructs developed for a specific purpose, of which the killer seems entirely unaware. One can but wonder why such killers' predecessors ate the symbolic apple of the Eden orchard, a taste for knowledge if, to this day, they abide in a state of such abysmal ignorance.

Luckily, we cannot kill the Energy of Life, the Individualization of the Universal Consciousness. Energy, as Einstein assured us, cannot be destroyed. What the killer destroys is not the miracle which I consider each body to be, but they terminate the purpose for which it has been created before it had a chance to fulfill its mission.

Let me repeat.

Perhaps Evelyn Monahan who, after the medical profession had given up, as a young lady managed to heal her blindness and other ailments, put it this way:

> *"I am a magnificent human being. I am without equal in all creation. My mind and body are so magnificently constructed that no feat of engineering could ever duplicate the uniqueness in myself. I will transcend all ordinary thinking and dwell entirely in my higher self".* [4]

To repeat, this is what we destroy when we kill a human being. Are you sure you can create anything even resembling such an 'engineering feat"?

Since every effect is preceded by its cause, just think what effect your killing will have on you. Remember Karma? That's all it is. There is no reward or punishment. There is only Cause and Effect. Rabbinical Judaism places Moses's lifetime somewhere between 1391–1271 BCE; although others give his date of birth as far back as 1571 BCE.

Sadly, his incredible insights did not protect him from wandering the desert of 40 years, although this biblical statement may also refer to "spiritual desert" rather then physical meandering. Perhaps it took that long to instill the precepts of the Decalogue in his people. We can but wander...

7
Thou shalt not commit adultery.

This, too, is directed more at the survival of the species than of individual members. While adultery could produce greater diversity, it is unlikely to raise the quality of parental care, which would assure the offspring's longevity. And longevity is of some importance because, more often then not, members of our species are less preoccupied with the material aspects of life in their more advanced years.

I might add that, in this respect, I speak from personal experience. I'd written more than 40 books since I retired from my profession. From tennis, skiing and other sports. From dancing, and partyingu all night.

We, humans, mature later in life, hence it pays us to have a stable domicile, which is hard to come be if we indulge in adultery.

8
Thou shalt not steal.

Once again, a first class recommendation for avoiding negative Karma. However, the concept of stealing can be, and hopefully has been, extended not only to material objects but also to ideas, concepts, and generally anything, which detracts the diversity to the Universe. We must never forget that the Universal Laws demand only one thing from us: to enhance the Universe by adding diversity to the phenomenal reality. No matter how seemingly transient, no matter how illusive. Without us, and without such as we are, the Universe would cease to expand.

That's our job.

That's our purpose.

9
Thou shalt not bear false witness against thy neighbour.

Thoughts are things. As already mentioned, they create reality. Lies detract from the enhancement of the illusion of our Universe. We are in the process of recreating a new Garden of Eden within our consciousness.

Regrettably, lies, accusations, falsehoods, and most certainly bearing false witness, demean the magnificent Potential within us. They all depreciate our ability to add, to contribute, to our reality. They are destructive, not constructive.

Moses observed what the concept of Egyptian gods did to people. They must have lived in fear of retribution of their gods.

And after all, your neighbour is an integral part of the group, eventually of the human species. Moses must have felt that the good of the many supersedes the good of the one. [5] In other words, that a deeper level we are all One.

This, as far as we can gather, is one of the fundamental precepts of the Universal Laws.

10

Thou shalt not covet thy neighbour's house, thou shalt not covet thy neighbour's wife, nor his manservant, nor his maidservant, nor his ox, nor his ass, nor any thing that is thy neighbour's.

This Commandment (as do all others) eliminates the need for police, jails. Strangely enough, there's not a single word about rewards or punishments. Strangely enough, even today we prefer the system created by Moses's 'predecessor', who produced the *Code of Hammurabi,* which, reputedly, Hammurabi received from the Babylonian god of justice. Like all codes that claim to have origin in a divine quarter, the Code introduces specific penalties, including physical punishments for the perpetrators.

In Mosaic Laws, people were expected to obey the laws *not* out of fear of retribution. Moses offered Laws that heightened people's consciousness. His people had been expected to obey the laws because it was the right thing to do, not out of fear.

Regrettably, most religions destroyed his highly educational method, and reverted to the carrot and the stick methodology, the ultimate nonsense of which were, and to this day are, eternal heaven and hell.

Hence, today, people do the 'right thing' only if they must, and they do the 'wrong thing' if they feel they'll get away with it.

We reached a most primitive, barbaric, pre Mosaic mentality.

~~~~~

So much for Moses' contribution to our ethics and morality. Sadly, we went down hill ever since. Our consciousness (artificial intelligence generated by our biological computer, i.e.: brain) did not evolve, but descended at an abysmal rate.

We are still in the kindergarten.

Luckily we are immortal.

As for Moses...

Reputedly he wondered the dessert for 40 years, endeavouring to instill his Commandments into his people. At least, he might have thought so. At long last he led his people across the Red Sea, to leave the emotional conditioning implanted by the Egyptians behind. The Red Sea symbolizes the freeing of his people from emotional ties to the Egyptian philosophy. In scriptures, colour red, invariably symbolizes emotions.

Yet it was a pyrrhic victory.

Not only he, himself, didn't sustain the high Consciousness offered him by his Higher Self on Mount Sinai, [6] but his people soon fell under the spell of newly evolved priesthood. In time, they developed Rabbinic Judaism.

*Pharisees claimed Mosaic authority for their interpretation of Jewish Laws, while **Sadducees** represented the authority of the priestly privileges and prerogatives established since the days of Solomon, when Zadok, their ancestor, officiated as High Priest.* [7]

After 40 years of wandering in the desert, **Moses** died within sight of the Promised Land on Mount Nebo. Perhaps coincidently, the Akkadian "nabu" means "to announce, prophesize", while Nebo was a Babylonian god of wisdom and agriculture, and a patron of scribes and schools. It seems that Moses had chosen not a bad place to die. He is said to have reached 120. Not bad considering that the longevity of Jews in his day and age was 40. On the other hand, as mentioned repeatedly, we are all immortal...

Moses has done the very best he could.

~~~~~~~~~

REFERENCES

(1) We must remember that we decide if we wish to be among the chosen Few.

(2) John 10:34

(3) *From Dake Annotated Reference Bible ©2007 by Dake Publishing. All rights reserved in U.S.A. and Other Countries.*

Forty-two Miracles by Moses

1. Moses' rod turned into a serpent
2. The serpent was transformed into a rod
3. Moses' hand was turned leprous
4. Moses' hand was healed of leprosy
5. The rod was turned into a serpent
6. The serpent was turned into a rod
7. Moses' hand was made leprous

8. Moses' hand was healed of leprosy
9. Moses' rod was turned into a serpent
   (Egyptian magicians also did so)
10. Moses' rod swallowed the others
11. The Nile River was changed into blood: first plague
    (Egyptian magicians also did so)
12. He created frogs: second plague
    (the magicians also did so)
13. He caused the frogs to die
14. He converted the dust to lice: third plague (the   magicians could not do this)
15. He created flies: fourth plague
16. He made Goshen exempt from flies
17. He removed the flies from Egypt
18. The murrain disease was imposed on Egyptian stock: fifth plague
19. The stock of Israel was exempt
20. He made boils from ashes: sixth plague
21. Hail and fire came: seventh plague
22. Goshen was exempt from the hail and fire
23. Moses stopped the hail and fire
24. Locusts descended: eighth plague)
25. The locusts were removed
26. Darkness came: ninth plague
27. Goshen was exempt from the total darkness
28. Death came to Egypt's firstborn: tenth plague
29. Israel's firstborn were exempt from death
30. Moses made a path through the Red Sea,   congealing the water
31. He melted the ice of Red Sea
32. The healing waters of Marah
33. Bread from heaven
34. Quail to eat
35. Water from the rock
36. His victory over Midian
37. He quenched the fire of death
38. The healing of Miriam
39. The earth swallowed the rebels
40. Moses stopped the plague
41. Water from the rock
42. The healing of Israel

"Sixteen other miracles that God performed when Moses was present:"

1. God's glory filling tabernacle (Ex 40:34).
2. Fire consuming sacrifices (Lev 9:24).
3. Fire killing priests (Lev 10:2).
4. The Fire which consumed some people (Num 11:2).
5. The fire was quenched (Num 11:2).
6. A month's supply of quails for about 6,000,000 people (Num 11:19-35).
7. The leprosy that was fixed upon Miriam (Num 12:10).
8. The healing of Miriam (Num 12:13-16).
9. The plague upon ten spies (Num 14:37).
10. The earth swallowed the rebels (Num 16:32).
11. The fire which consumed some people (Num 16:35).
12. The plague which killed 14,700 people (Num 16:49).
13. Aaron's rod that bore almonds (Num 17:8).
14. Water from the rock (Num 20:11).
15. The healing of Israel (Num 21:5-9).
16. The plague that killed 24,000 people

(4) Evelyn Monahan: *"The Miracle of Metaphysical Healing."* Parker Publishing Co. Inc. 1975

(5) https://geekychristian.com/evidence-the-temple-was-not-gods-will/

(6) With the possible exception or Nathan, who appears to oscillates between David and his Higher Self. One cannot always rely on scribes who wrote and rewrote the scriptures to the instructions given by the priesthood. To date, the more than 450 translations of the Bible provide ample evidence!

(7) This theme is explored at length in my historical novel *PETER & PAUL.*

(4) Once the nature of hermaphroditic Adam was split into two sexes, Eve symbolized his indispensible subconscious (sometimes referred to as soul). Now we know, of course, that both sexes are equipped with both halves of the brain, although both sexes tend to favour the use of one side or the other.

(5) Amusingly, this concept has been adopted and expressed in the 1982 Sci-Fi film named The Wrath of Khan, of the Star Trek series. Spock (the 1st officer) says, "Logic clearly

dictates that the needs of the many outweigh the needs of the few." Captain Kirk answers, "Or the one."

(6) A "mount", in scriptures, always symbolizes a raised state of Consciousness, such as we are expected to achieve during prayer.

(7) https://www.google.com/search?client=firefox-b-d&q=Pharases+and+Sedducees

A Word about the Author

Stanisław Kapuściński (aka **Stan I.S. Law**), architect, sculptor and prolific writer, was educated in Poland and England. Since 1965 he has resided in Canada. His special interests cover a broad spectrum of arts, sciences and philosophy. His fiction and non-fiction attest to his particular passion for the scope and the development of Human Potential. He has authored more than forty books, twenty of them novels.

Under his real name, he published non-fiction books sharing his vision of reality. He also composed two collections of poems in his original native tongue in which he satirizes his view of the world while paying homage to Bozena Happach's sculptures.

~~~~~

By the same author

Non-fiction

VISUALIZATION—Creating your own Universe
KEY TO IMMORTALITY
[Commentary on the Gospel of Thomas]
BEYOND RELIGION I
BEYOND RELIGION II
BEYOND RELIGION III
[Each volume contains 52 Essays on Perception of Reality]
DICTIONARY OF BIBLICAL SYMBOLISM
VICIOUS CIRCLE (Volumes 1 to 6)
[In search of Secular Ethics]
DELUSIONS—Pragmatic Realism
CONCLUSIONS—Pragmatic Reality
PSALM 23 — Exegesis
ISAIAH —The Birth of Higher Consciousness
THE LORD'S PRAYER
SELF EGO VIRUS

~~~~~~~

Fiction by Stan I.S. Law
(aka Stanisław Kapuściński)
Novels

WALL—Love, Sex & Immortality [Aquarius Trilogy Book I]
PLUTO EFFECT [Aquarius Trilogy Book II]
OLYMPUS — Of Gods and Men [Aquarius Trilogy Book III]
MARVIN CLARK—In Search of Freedom
GIFT OF GAMMAN
ENIGMA OF THE SECOND COMING
ONE JUST MAN [Winston Trilogy Book I]
ELOHIM—Masters & Minions [Winston Trilogy Book II]
WINSTON'S KINGDOM [Winston Trilogy Book III]
THE AVATAR SYNDROME [Avatar Trilogy Book I]
HEADLESS WORLD [Avatar Trilogy Book II]
AWAKENING [Avatar Trilogy Book III]
THE PRINCESS
ALEC [Alexander Trilogy Book I]
ALEXANDER [Alexander Trilogy Book II]
SACHA—The Way Back [Alexander Trilogy Book III]
YESHUA—Personal Memoir of the Missing Years of Jesus
THE GATE—Things my Mother told Me
NOW—Being and Becoming
ALEXANDER TRILOGY
AVATAR TRILOGY
AQUARIUS TRILOGY
WINSTON TRILOGY

Anthologies of Short Stories

THE JEWEL
CATS and DOGS Series
SCI-FI 1
SCI-FI 2

Poetry in Polish

KILKA SŁÓW I TROCHĘ GLINY
WIĘCEJ SŁÓW I WIĘCEJ GLINY

www.ingramcontent.com/pod-product-compliance
Lightning Source LLC
Chambersburg PA
CBHW030311030426
42337CB00012B/672